BOOK ANALYSIS

Written
Translate

The Grapes of Wrath

BY JOHN STEINBECK

Bright
≡Summaries.com

JOHN STEINBECK

AMERICAN WRITER

- **Born in Salinas (California) in 1902**
- **Died in New York in 1968**
- **Notable works:**
  - *Of Mice and Men* (1937), novel
  - *The Grapes of Wrath* (1939), novel
  - *East of Eden* (1952), novel

John Steinbeck (1902-1968) was an American writer whose novels (*Of Mice and Men*, 1937; *The Grapes of Wrath*, 1939; *East of Eden*, 1952, etc.) share two similarities: they are set in his native California and they talk of the difficult living conditions of the rural populations. A reporter for the *International Herald Tribune* during World War II, Steinbeck received the Nobel Prize in Literature in 1962. Several of his novels have been adapted for the cinema and contributed to his popularity.

THE GRAPES OF WRATH

A REVOLUTIONARY NOVEL

- **Genre:** novel
- **Reference edition:** Steinbeck, J. (2016) *The Grapes of Wrath*. Maryland: Hamilton Books.
- **First edition:** 1939
- **Themes:** hunger, poverty, support, migration, revolt, work

The Grapes of Wrath is a novel published in 1939, set in the United States during the crisis of 1929, which caused the most severe consequences for farmers. The novel follows the story of a poor family of sharecroppers, the Joads, who are forced to leave Oklahoma and their land due to the disastrous climatic conditions, the stock market crash and the industrialization of agriculture. They leave for California, thinking they will be able to find land and work there. However, the Joads and thousands more Okies (natives of Oklahoma) meet nothing more than hostility from the indigenous in the West, along with poverty and hunger. Still, the men do not give up and help each other to the end.

SUMMARY

THE END OF THE CROP SHARE

At a ball, when drunk, Tom Joad kills a man. When he is released from prison for good behavior, he decides to join his father, a corn farmer, and his family: his grandparents, Ma, Al, Noah, Rose of Sharon, Winfield and Ruthie. He makes the journey with pastor Casy. On arriving, the two men meet the representatives of the owners who have come to announce the end of crop sharing (a mode of farming in which the owner of a country estate leases his land to farmers, sharecroppers, who undertake to cultivate and share the harvest with him) and its replacement by the tractor which is worth, in returns, the work of a dozen families. Following a decision of the bank, the tenants must leave. The machines are even ordered to tear down the houses to ensure that the occupants leave.

When Tom finds his family at Uncle John's home, his father tells him that everyone is leaving for California. The area has a reputation as a haven for sharecroppers expelled from their property. There will be an abundance of work and life there will be idyllic: "We had hard times here. 'Course it'll be all different out there - plenty work, an' ever'thing nice an' green, an' little white houses an' oranges growin' aroun'" (Chapter 10). However, they are still ignorant of the fact that the place is certainly beautiful, but they are not permitted to touch a single fruit harvested when picking or to put even a finger on the white houses. To be able to leave, the family must sell their furniture and personal belongings at ridiculous prices in order to buy a truck. Casy accompanies them, even if this means having to feed another mouth and cramming another person into the truck: the Joads are not ones to refuse guests.

FALSE HOPE

The road to California proves difficult because of the heat, lack of water and the truck's state of disrepair. It also proves fatal for Grandfather, who dies from a heart attack caused by the forced abandonment of his land. Along the way, the Joads meet the Wilsons and decide to complete the rest of their journey together and to help one another.

But during their journey they meet men who are returning from California and tell them that, in reality, there are no jobs in the West: there is no land available, owners are clinging to it with fervor and fear newcomers who might steal their jobs. Over there, women and children from the East are starving, and the men, continually threatened by the local authorities, are feared and hated. The pamphlets handed out in the East are a scam put in place to attract people, rob them of their belongings and exploit them.

In a camp, Tom converses with another expatriate who explains why these brochures were sent: the amount of fruit that needs to be harvested as soon as possible to avoid their rotting is so high that at least three thousand people are needed. But over six thousand people arrived ready to battle one another and accept any conditions in order to get work. With such a large workforce, the harvest was quickly completed.

Therefore, Noah refuses to continue with the journey and stops on the riverbank. In addition, Wilson's wife is sick and too weak to go on: the two families must part ways. Furthermore, Grandma dies.

Shortly after, men arrive at the camp: they are hiring men on behalf of the farmer Tulare. Floyd, a man of the camp, requires a specific number of employees with fixed wages, i.e. real working conditions. But following this claim, the sheriff, seeking to prevent a possible revolt, gets out of his car and forces Floyd to leave on the basis of made-up motives. Threats are being increasingly exchanged: if the men do not go to work, the camp will be set on fire. Floyd frees himself from his bonds and beats the men, then he flees. Four gunmen arrive to help the sheriff. Casy takes responsibility for the beatings in order to protect his own. He is taken away.

THE GOVERNMENT CAMP

Connie, the father of Rose of Sharon's unborn child, abandons his family while the Joads hit the road in the hope of finding a place in the government camp. There, things are happening just like the rumors are saying: they are finally treated like human beings. The camp is run and managed by the residents themselves and entry is prohibited to the police.

However, the authorities are seeking men to create riots inside the camp so that they can use the excuse that workers are unable to govern themselves and that external policy is necessary. Closing the camps where the Okies are respected is their priority, as men who regain their dignity are a danger.

The lack of work in the region finally pushes the Joads to leave. They resume their journey and are directed towards picking peaches on the Hoopers' farm. When they arrive, they find that the barracks are dirty and the shop only sells food that is out of their price range. But they have no choice and settle there.

THE REVOLT

Tom, puzzled by the high number of guards outside, decides to take a walk and meets Casy. He and other men are on strike to protest against the low wages. During the discussion, armed men arrive and attack the strikers who they refer to as "dirty reds". Things go wrong and one of them violently strikes Casy, who dies of his injuries. In a rage, Tom knocks out a guard, but is beaten in turn. He returns with a broken nose and a swollen face. He is now forced to hide. The Joad family decides to leave.

Shortly after, they find work in cotton fields where the conditions are not too bad. There are wagons in which they are housed and the possibility of daily meat servings. However, staying is too dangerous for Tom who is being actively sought by the police throughout the region, and, his crime having been revealed by Ruthie, he is obliged to leave once again. He plans to carry on Casy's fight.

Rain falls continuously throughout the region. The tents of the emigrants are flooded and storms are forcing families to leave for the cities. These hordes of starving people first provoke the pity of the city dwellers, then their fear and hatred. The lack of food makes the Okies prepared to lose all dignity, to steal and to lie just for a crumb of bread. The fear of death soon turns into anger.

Rose of Sharon gives birth to a dead child. The rain does not stop, and the water level rises, threatening to fill the wagon. They must leave, but Al decides to stay with the Wainwrights close to their daughter Aggie, whom he met during their stay and whom he intends to marry. Ma, Pa, Uncle John, Rose of Sharon and the children go to a barn for shelter. A man and his son have already taken refuge there. The man is dying for lack of food. Following a look from Ma, Rose of Sharon understands that her mother is asking her to offer her breast to the starving man. They all leave the room and the young woman does so, with a smile.

CHARACTER STUDY

MA

The mother has no first name, and is immediately found to have a strong character and immense goodness. Ma Joad is indestructible, brave and tenacious. She proves this during the episode of the grandmother's death, among other moments: she stays alone at her side all night without telling anyone, for fear that the death would jeopardize the trip. She knows how to be silent and restrained in order to protect her own. For the same purpose, she can also be violent: this is the case when she grabs a jack and threatens her husband to prevent the family from separating (Tom and Casy wanted to leave them because of a breakdown and re-join them in California). Ma manifests the intractability of her character and her authority. Otherwise, she is modest and does not show her emotions, again for the sake of her family. Moreover, Ma upholds the dignity of the Joad family: at the government camp, she ensures that everyone is dressed up to the nines for the visit of the women's committee.

Steinbeck portrays an archetypal mother who holds ancestral values and appears to be the protective guardian of the home and the family unit. Nonetheless, Ma Joad recognizes the limits of her function, which is to ensure daily subsistence, when she says: "That's all I can do. I can't do no more. All the rest'd get upset if I done any more'n that" (Chapter 13). But she also guarantees the spiritual nourishment by opposing her family, who do not wish for pastor Casy to joint them due to the lack of space and food: a pastor can always help. She therefore embodies a certain wisdom.

ROSE OF SHARON

Her name comes from the *Song of Songs*: "I am a rose of Sharon, a lily of the valleys" (II, 1). Rose is the embodiment of motherhood. She is blonde with a soft face and a voluptuous body. Her only concern is for the child she carries within her. All external events are interpreted by the young woman as divine signs: the sudden death of the family dog resonates as a sign of the impending death of her child. Rose often shows herself to be childish and naïve. For example, when Connie leaves and she believes that he has gone to find books to study. She is also fearful and withdrawn, and she complains incessantly. Yet, at the end of the novel, she acquires nobility.

TOM

Tom is the prodigal son, but he is also the most fragile. Sentenced to seven years in prison but released after four years for good behavior, Tom has already killed a man. His illegal situation makes him a danger to his family. Indeed, his parole does not allow him to cross borders. In addition, Tom, who bears the least humiliation and injustice, frequently pushes his limits with local authorities: nothing is more important to him than dignity, which the sheriffs seek to take from him. The killing or Casy's murderer finally condemns him to hiding.

His speech is interesting and contains the words of the former pastor, adopting a pantheistic vision of the world, ruled by a supreme soul: there is a gigantic soul that is common to all. This mysticism allows him to expect to continue to share the life of his family in a diffuse and invisible way. Tom also wants to concentrate on collective action and open the family to the community.

ANALYSIS

A DIFFICULT HISTORICAL CONTEXT

Steinbeck gives an account of the intolerable reality of the lives of migrant workers coming to the West to work as seasonal fruit pickers.

The economic crisis

The novel is set during the Great Depression, also known as the crisis of 1929. At that time, the effects of unemployment were disastrous, with a large portion of the population suffering from malnutrition.

The novel highlights in particular the hard gaze focused on the poor in the United States. Indeed, the American individualist tradition considers poverty as the outcome of a natural inclination to laziness. Therefore, before the introduction of the New Deal (economic and social reform motion in the US in 1933), public and private support were distributed sparingly and at the expense of humiliation, in order to deter people from resorting to them. For example, in order to benefit from aid, there must have been a prior thorough search of the person's home in order to verify the lack of resources, and the American newspapers often used vexatious titles for the poor, such as "welfare fraud" or "cheaters of the help to the unemployed". Everything was in place to make the poor feel ashamed and unworthy.

The West

The West was seen as an area of freedom due to the extent of its virgin land. These vacant lands pushed the Western man towards individualism. This place where everyone could own a farm by simply settling there naturally generated economic and political equality; individual freedom and equality were the values that prevailed. Thus, the man of the West no longer supported the legal constraints and each maintained order by applying his own justice, or by partnering with other Western people. The Western man's ideal was the freedom for each individual to make his own destiny and he refused any organized politics or rational methods of the government.

However, things changed when the dry lands were reached. It was no longer possible to take possession of land in order to operate with the old methods of isolated farming. It became necessary to implement expensive irrigation works and unlock capitals too considerable for a single farmer. The nature of the territory thus required overcoming individualism in favor of the social. Thus was born a spirit of enterprise and adventure that led to rapid industrial development.

Migration

"Highway 66 is the main migrant road. [...] 66 is the path of people in flight, refugees from dust and shrinking land, from the thunder of tractors and shrinking ownership, from the desert's slow northward invasion, from the twisting winds that howl up out of Texas, from the floods that bring no richness to the land and steal what little richness is there. From all of these the people are in flight, and they come into 66 from the tributary side roads, from the wagon tracks and the rutted country roads. 66 is the mother road, the road of flight" (Chapter 12).

The Dust Bowl drought (an expression that refers to the area from Texas to South Dakota which was invaded by dust storms in 1933), as well as the end of sharecropping and its replacement with industrialized agriculture, forced families to flee to the West. At the time of harvest, 150,000 migrants were travelling through California, destitute and homeless. The locals reproached their ignorance and dirtiness and welcomed them with hostility, disparagingly calling them *Okies* and equating them to chimpanzees, highlighting the rejection of misery and poverty, which was then related to a lack of merit. These seasonal workers fell into servitude and did not even have the right to vote.

Steinbeck, as a committed journalist, described the difficult living conditions of these men forced into nomadism: they stayed in makeshift camps called "Hoovervilles" (referring to President Hoover who was in office at the time) that were comparable to slums, they were victims of malnutrition, caught various diseases, etc. They underwent a process of progressive dehumanization. Furthermore, the farmers, for fear of revolt, had their installations guarded by trigger-happy armed militia. However, in 1932, the federal government of Franklin Roosevelt wanted to help these debased workers: fifteen camps were created, in which quality sanitary facilities were installed in order to give the men back their dignity. In addition, these communities were managed by the residents themselves, according to the principles of socialism.

In his articles, Steinbeck proposed solutions: the gift of agricultural land to emigrants and the establishment of seasonal workforce planning at the site of the harvest in order to curb the massive displacement phenomenon and the wage decrease that accompanied it.

FROM HUNGER TO ANGER

Food plays an essential role in this rural world that possesses only the bare necessities: it symbolizes the human drama.

The allusions to food are numerous throughout the novel: "Ma opened the oven and took out the pile of roasted bones, crisp and brown, with plenty of gnawing meat left" (Chapter 13); "Ma passed the boiled potatoes out and brought the half sack from the tent and put it with the pan of pork" (Chapter 18); "Ma sliced salt pork into her second frying pan" (Chapter 28), etc. The mother aspires to recreate a home through her cooked meals. Indeed, good food is associated with the heat of a family gathered under the same roof, as opposed to industrial food: "sandwiches wrapped in waxed paper, white bread, pickle, cheese, Spam, a piece of pie branded like an engine part. He ate without relish" (Chapter 5). Steinbeck also denounces this chain-made food to feed the men who, due to the mediation of the machine, the tractor, are no longer attached to the nourishing earth that is now foreign to them:

> "And this is easy and efficient. So easy that the wonder goes out of work, so efficient that the wonder goes out of

land and the working of it, and with the wonder the deep understanding and the relation. [...] But the machine man, driving a dead tractor on land he does not know and love, understands only chemistry; and he is contemptuous of the land and of himself" (Chapter 11).

Defeating hunger becomes the main concern for the Joad family; this is why pork, the symbol of satisfied appetite, haunts conversations. This lack of food also causes the disruption of behavior since hunger makes people selfish: at the beginning of the novel, a tractor driver gives Tom a ride and Tom points out to him that, in order for him to feed his family with his tractor, fifteen other families die of hunger. The hungry men are forced to forget their duty of solidarity to buy food and must fight simply to survive. But Ma does not only fight for her family: she also fulfills her nurturing duty to the children she encounters in the Hoovervilles.

However, although hunger weakens man, it also plants in him a feeling of revolt because a man who has experienced hunger is no longer afraid: "How can you frighten a man whose hunger is not only in his own cramped stomach but in the wretched bellies of his children? You can't scare him—he has known a fear beyond every other" (Chapter 19). The insurrection of the famished is therefore perceived as irremediable and almost organic: "And the anger began to ferment" (Chapter 21). Everything happens as if it were a chemical reaction, where hunger can cause nothing other than anger. This is seen positively, as a feeling that brings individuals together, unlike the hunger that disrupts a community through selfishness. It is a sign of vitality, proof that there is still enough energy to get out of oppression, or even find a cure for depression: "And where a number of men gathered together, the fear went from their faces, and anger took its place. And the women sighed with relief, for they knew it was all right - the break had not come; and the break would never come as long as fear could turn to wrath" (Chapter 29).

THE BIRTH OF A COMMUNITY

The forced exodus of the Joad family causes the slow erosion of the family structure. The mother insists on the importance of maintaining the family unity and solidarity that binds its members: "All we got is the family unbroke" (Chapter 16). Ma is aware of the hazards of uprooting: "They was the time when we was on the lan'. They was a boundary to us then. Ol' folks died off, an' little fellas come, an' we was always one thing—we was the fambly—kinda whole and clear. An' now we ain't clear no more" (Chapter 25).

On the other hand, the disintegration of the family means the joining of the nomad community. It starts with the joining of the Joads with the Wilsons, on the death of the grandfather: during this difficult event the Wilsons share their bible and blanket. The strict family circle is thus broken in favor of the notion of a large family community: "In the evening a strange thing happened: the twenty families became one family, the children were the children of all. The loss of home became one loss, and the golden time in the West was one dream" (Chapter 17). The families gather around campfires and become one big tribe. Through this, Steinbeck represents the force of human unity and celebrates the adaptability that he sees as specific to the human species: "Thus they changed their social life - changed as in the whole universe only man can change" (Chapter 17). The final scene is particularly representative of the abolition of family boundaries, since Rose of Sharon's milk, produced for her dead child, is used to save a stranger.

PHILOSOPHICAL REFERENCES

The Supreme Soul (Ralph Waldo Emerson)

Ralph Waldo Emerson (American writer and philosopher, 1803-1882) developed an idealist philosophy which states that the individual is able to enter into an intimate resonance with nature.

More specifically, the idea is echoed by Casy and later by Tom. The human soul animates and controls all the human organs, it is not a simple function or simply an option, it is that on which everything rests. It is vast and one cannot control it; while we are nothing, it is everything. The soul makes the intelligence of man genius, makes his will a virtue and makes his affection love. It sublimes all the aspects of man. This philosophy encourages the awareness that man is nothing, and that he must obey the soul or pure nature, in order to allow himself to be guided by it and what is beyond it.

Pragmatism (William James)

The empirical philosophy of William James (American philosopher, 1842-1910), pragmatism, is based on the idea that knowledge gives rise to different experiences, and comes from a wandering movement through intermediary experiences.

A link can be established between pragmatism and the migrant workers who are eager to reach the West: these 'hobos' are an integral part of the American capitalist economy, characterized by alternating booms and crises. This economy heavily uses the concepts of hiring and firing of the workforce. The seasonal worker is the march towards knowledge. In other words, he symbolizes the passage from one experience to another, from traditional agriculture to industrialized agriculture: from the experience of the first pioneer communities of the West, equal, free and individualistic, to the experience of industrialization made necessary by the nature of the territory when the fertile lands have all been exploited and when it becomes necessary to resort to the community (for practical and financial reasons) in order to exploit the remaining resources.

East vs. West

The opposition between the East and the West is symbolic:

- The East embodies history, art and literature. The man who goes eastward is walking the path of his ancestors;
- The West represents the future and the spirit of adventure and enterprise. The road to the West is relative to the migratory instinct of birds and quadrupeds. These natural phenomena also affect nations and individuals at certain times in the story.

FURTHER REFLECTION

SOME QUESTIONS TO THINK ABOUT...

- What links can be established between *The Grapes of Wrath* and *Idylle*, a novel by Guy de Maupassant?
- What is the role of the Joads truck in the novel?
- In what sense is *The Grapes of Wrath* a development of the pastoral myth?
- Highlight extracts in Steinbeck's work that illustrate the phenomenon of devaluation.
- To what biblical resonances does the title of the novel refer?
- How does the film adaptation of *The Grapes of Wrath* differ from the book?
- *The Grapes of Wrath* has also been an influence in music. Give examples and discuss them.
- What can be said about the role of men in the novel?
- Develop the theme of "the reds" in the novel.
- Why does Ma try several times to make her husband angry?

We want to hear from you!
Leave a comment on your online library
and share your favourite books on social media!

FURTHER READING

REFERENCE EDITION

- Steinbeck, J. (2016) *The Grapes of Wrath*. Maryland: Hamilton Books.

REFERENCE STUDIES

- Lemardeley-Cunci, M.-C. (1998) *Les Raisins de la colère de John Steinbeck*. Paris: Gallimard.

ADAPTATIONS

- *The Grapes of Wrath*. (1940) [Film]. John Ford. Dir. USA: Twentieth Century Fox Film Corporation.

MORE FROM BRIGHTSUMMARIES.COM

- Reading guide – *Of Mice and Men* by John Steinbeck
- Reading guide – *The Pearl* by John Steinbeck

www.brightsummaries.com

Ebook EAN: 9782806271198

Paperback EAN: 9782806271204

Legal Deposit: D/2015/12603/487

Cover: © Primento

Digital conception by Primento, the digital partner of publishers.

Printed in Great Britain
by Amazon